Department of the Environment
Ancient Monuments and Historic Buildings

Bury St Edmunds Abbey

SUFFOLK

A. B. WHITTINGHAM MA, ARIBA, FSA

A revised and shortened version of an article published in volume CVIII of the *Archaeological Journal*

LONDON: HER MAJESTY'S STATIONERY OFFICE

ISBN 0 11 670412 8

Contents

History

King's shrine, and cradle of the law

The abbey of Bury St Edmunds occupies a site which has been in religious use from the early seventh century. In about 633 King Sigebert, the first Christian king of the East Angles, settled a religious community here entering it himself till summoned to repel the heathen, when he was slain, bearing his wand in battle against the Mercians under King Penda. To this place, then known as Bedericsworth, were brought in 903 the remains of King Edmund, who had been martyred by the Danes in 870. The intervening years had seen the issue of the remarkable St Edmund memorial coinage, which would have both spread patriotic fervour and served as a stimulus to remove the saint's body to a royal monastery. He had been slain by Danish arrows and decapitated at Haegelisdun (Hellesdon by Norwich, rather than the Norman alternatives Hoxne and Sutton) where the first miracle took place, so often represented in art, when a wolf crying 'here' led to the recovery of his head. The acquisition of so notable a relic as this royal saint was to make the monastery a place of pilgrimage as well as a recipient of numerous royal grants. Ultimately, Bury St Edmunds was to become one of the five richest Benedictine monasteries in England.

In 945, or shortly after, the land surrounding Bedericsworth was given to the community by Edmund, son of Edward the Elder. With the renewal of Danish raids St Edmund's body was in 1010 taken for safety to London where it remained three years. After its return Sweyn made demands for ransom from St Edmund's lands, but his sudden death by 'the Saint's spear' when his demands were refused brought increasing respect for the saint's power. To atone for Sweyn's impiety his son, King Canute, added a rotunda to the earlier church of St Mary in 1020 while Bishop Ailwin granted freedom from episcopal control and substituted twenty monks from St Benet's near Horning and from Ely for the secular priests. Even Edward I dreamed that St Edmund was making another Sweyn of him, when he started infringing monastic rights in the town outside the abbey. Edward the Confessor granted a mint in 'St Edmund's Bury', the first use of this name.

After the Norman Conquest, Bishop Arfast attempted to turn the abbey church into his cathedral, but in 1081 this scheme was defeated when William the Conqueror confirmed the freedom of the abbey from episcopal control. The same underlying guilt that inspired the

St Edmund coinage produced the outburst of Norman church building and the size of their greater churches. This is shown more particularly in the scale of the new abbey church here at Bury, preparations for which could now begin so as to accommodate sixty additional monks. From the chronicles of the period it is possible to obtain an account of the progress of the work in considerable detail. 'In the time of Abbot Baldwin [1065–97] first Thurstan, afterwards Tolin, undertook the office of Sacrist. These two, in the time of the said Abbot, when the ancient timber church had been levelled, laid the foundations of our church, erected walls, completed the presbytery in full, and arranged the translation of the Blessed Martyr.' The translation ceremony took place in 1095 and was attended by Bishop Walkelin of Winchester and by Ralph Flambard, the royal chaplain, afterwards bishop of Durham. Building construction probably began shortly before 1090. Most of the stone came from Barnack, being conveyed by boat from Gunwade. The poet John Lydgate, c 1430, says that some of Baldwin's work was built with:

Stone brought from Kane (Caen) out of Normandye
By the Se, and set up on the Strande at Ratylsdene,
and carried forth be lande.

Tolin was succeeded by Godfrey, who completed fully the refectory, chapter house, infirmary and abbot's hall. He also obtained a great bell, which implies that the central tower of the church was nearly ready for it. Robert II, acting abbot from 1102, died a month after his consecration in 1107. Meanwhile, 'he caused the Cloister, Chapter House, Refectory, Dormitory and his Camera to be built'. Between 1107 therefore, and the appointment of the next sacrist (in 1121?), Godfrey built the infirmary—in use before the crypt was dedicated in 1114—followed by the transepts, the central tower to roof level and two bays of the nave to full height to support the tower and to house the choir. His work included also a fifth bay to the presbytery to accommodate the crypt entrances and transept aisles. His transepts, also of five bays, have few parallels, and the combination of an aisle with projecting chapels as well is equally unusual. 'Two men of complete prudence followed him (Godfrey), Ralph and Hervey, sacrists in the time of Abbot Anselm [1120–48]. They built the circuit of the walls round the forecourt of the church, the church of the Blessed Mary with its tower . . . and the Tower of St James. . . .' Before his death in 1142 Bishop John of Rochester dedicated the apsidal flanking chapel or

'Porticus of St Faith ... over the Porticus of St Denis.' This suggests that by that time, apart from the clerestory where Norman work ends at the break over the stair turret doors, the nave and west transept were virtually complete, though the west front with its three great arches was without the three towers.

In the middle of the twelfth century new building operations received a set-back when a serious fire *c* 1150 damaged the abbots' hall, refectory, dormitory, chapter house and the old House of the Infirm. These buildings were repaired and reroofed during the remainder of the time of Abbot Ording (1148–56). The great west front, the most substantial portion of the abbey church surviving today, as completed under Abbot Samson, 1182–1211, had a 'major tower' placed centrally over the west transept, and a lower octagonal tower at each end, probably rising two stages above the clerestory. The chronicler Jocelin recorded the progress of this work in great detail. Samson as subsacrist during the vacancy of the abbacy (1180–82) collected a vast store of stone and sand for building the tower. When questioned, he said that burgesses had given him money for building and finishing it. He 'completed one storey in the major West Tower.' His sacrist Hugo 'completed the Great Tower towards the west, placing the roof and leading it, the lord Samson supplying the ceiling and beams, and whatever woodwork there is there. Also he fully completed as to stonework the Tower next to the Chapel of St Faith, one storey being completed in the other Tower next to the Chapel of St Catharine.' His successor as sacrist, Walter de Banham (*c* 1200–11) 'fully completed the Great Tower which is next to the Chapel of St Faith, placing the spire on it, which lord Hugo the sacrist had completed as to walling.' Jocelin adds that Geoffrey Ridel, bishop of Ely, requested Samson to let him have oaks for his own building operations. Samson, not wishing to offend the bishop agreed, but immediately felled 'for the steeple of the Great Tower' the best oaks at Elmsett which Geoffrey had intended and had secretly marked. This gives an indication of the competition between the two great west fronts of Ely Cathedral and Bury Abbey, both rising during the same decade.

Abbot Samson also found time to improve his own accommodation and that of his guests. Sometime before 1200 Hugo the Sacrist completed a new guest hall, presumably the Black Hostry, to relieve the pressure of guests. After the completion of this new guest-house for Benedictine monks, Abbot Samson built a new house, later known as

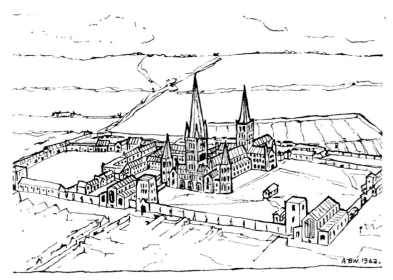

the Hall of Pleas, for himself and the most important guests, and shortly afterwards reconstructed the original abbot's house as a guest house for those who were not monks and had brought fewer than fourteen horses.

Abbot Samson is perhaps best remembered not for his building activity but for his friendship with both Henry II and Richard I. In 1181, Henry II visited Bury, and during his stay there refused the eager Samson permission to accompany him on the crusade. When Richard I was held a prisoner in Germany, Samson took an active part in raising the ransom money, and journeyed to visit the King, taking with him many gifts. One of Richard's first acts upon his return to England in 1194 was to make a thanksgiving visit to Bury Abbey. Richard's successor, John, visited Bury too and, after Samson's death in 1211, kept the office of the abbot vacant in order to appropriate the revenues. After much trouble, culminating in an appeal to Rome by the convent, John was forced to confirm the election of Hugh Northwold in 1215. In the meantime, Bury Abbey played a significant part in the wider troubles of King John's reign. On 20 November 1214, the earls and barons assembled in the abbey church to listen to Archbishop Langton, who read them Henry I's charter. Each swore on the high altar that unless the King granted similar liberties they would go to war against him. As a direct result of this meeting Magna Carta was sealed eventually by

King John on 15 June 1215. Under Abbot Hugh Northwold (1215–29), structural activities were largely confined to enlarging the little parlour, where necessary conversation was allowed, and rebuilding the chapter house, which was narrowed and lengthened. This involved moving the prior's house and other alterations nearby. A collapse of part of the central tower in 1210 was not serious enough to prevent another bell being added after the repair.

Throughout the thirteenth century, the abbey continued to prosper, though relations with the townspeople, who resented the authority of the abbot and convent, were rarely cordial. A new larger abbot's palace was begun near the river when in the later years of his reign Henry III visited the abbey several times. In 1275 the surviving centre of Canute's rotunda and the adjacent transeptal chapel of St Mary were pulled down and replaced by the large Lady Chapel flanking the presbytery, while opposite it on the south a shorter narrower chapel was provided for St Botolph. Towards the end of the century, a Charnel Chapel was built in the centre of the Great Cemetery to house the excessive number of bones which were accumulating in the over-crowded graveyard. The fourteenth century was to be an eventful one for the abbey. The numerous disputes between the abbey and the townspeople reached a climax in the celebrated riots of 1327, when the burgesses sought to obtain civic independence. These riots lasted for most of the summer and resulted in the sacking and burning of a large proportion of the abbey, the abduction of the abbot to Brabant, and the slaying of several monks. In addition at least thirteen of the manor houses belonging to the abbey were burned, and animals to the value of £6000 were carried off. Peace was finally effected, the townspeople being heavily fined. A later dispute involving the abbey lasted from 1345 to 1350 when the bishop of Norwich sought to annul the abbey's exemption from diocesan control. The attempt ended in failure. In 1379 Abbot John of Brinkley died, and the prior and convent elected as his successor John of Timworth, the sub-prior. Pope Urban VI put forward his own nominee for the post, Edward Bromefield, a monk. The ensuing dispute dragged on for five years, and ended with the pope agreeing to the election of John Timworth, who commanded the majority of local support. In 1381 the abbey was again plundered during the disturbance associated with Jack Straw's rebellion. Goods and treasure to the value of £1000 were seized by the mob and among those murdered at the abbey were the prior and

An east prospect of the Abbey by Samuel and Nathaniel Buck, 1741. This shows
St Mary's Church, the sacrist's house, Abbey church in front of
St James's Queen's Chamber, Great Gate, dovecot and mill, with
infirmary and prior's house over fish ponds and vineyard in the foreground

Sir John Cavendish, the chief justice. As a result the town was out-
lawed and fined 2000 marks. This and other disasters all involved
further building operations, one of the more important being a new
campanile above the choir, built at a cost of £866 13s 4d, after the
spire had been blown down in the great gale of 1361. This undoubtedly
included a timber spire as well as the heightening of the tower. In it
was hung a great bell, weighing 3.5t. New upper windows were
provided round St Edmund's shrine, and the nave ceiling was painted
to match that further east. John of Gaunt gave seven glass windows,
and his son Thomas Beaufort, Duke of Exeter, the one time Lord
Chancellor, was buried in the Lady Chapel (in 1427).

The fifteenth century began with some danger of another encroach-
ment on monastic rights when Archbishop Arundel paid a visit to the
abbey in 1400. He was received with due respect but it was made quite
clear to him that this was not accepted as an official Visitation and
inquiry into the conduct of the monastery. Another visit was that of
Henry VI, who gave eight weeks' notice of his intention to spend
Christmas at the abbey in 1433. In fact he stayed for four months after
Abbot Curteys (1429–46) had set eighty men to work improving and
repairing his palace. In 1446 Parliament met in the refectory to try

Humphrey Duke of Gloucester, but the trial never took place as he was found dead in suspicious circumstances at St Saviour's Hospital outside the north gate of the town on the day after his arrest. Thereafter the political importance of the abbey declined, and the King's Hall had been converted into 'quite a good granary' by 1465.

Meanwhile the present church of St Mary had been built by the parishioners between 1425 and 1433 in the south-west corner of the Great Cemetery, on the site of its Norman predecessor; and the congregation narrowly escaped disaster as they were still using the abbey nave, when in 1430 the south side of the west tower collapsed. In 1431 the east side followed, so that Abbot William Curteys was faced with further unwelcome expense. Next year the north side was deliberately felled on the advice of Thomas Mapilton, the King's master mason. A papal bull granting indulgences for the repair of the 'clocher' estimated the cost of repairs at 60 000 ducats (£27 000), and in 1435 repair work seems to have begun in earnest, and continued until 1465.

In that year, 1465, the plumbers left a brazier burning on the west tower during their lunch. In their absence, a wind arose and in consequence the whole church and refectory were burnt out, the 'great pinnacle,' or spire, subsided into the crossing, the fleche of the palace

was burned, and the abbot's chapel collapsed. The necessary repairs were extensive and included the insertion of vaulting, to make the church more fire-resistant, and the building of a western spire which was not completed till after 1506. Various bequests towards the repair and embellishing of the abbey church occur at intervals in the meantime.

The later years of the abbey's existence appear to have been among the more tranquil in its history. In 1533, Mary Tudor, Queen of France and sister of Henry VIII, was buried here in great state, but her body had soon to be removed from the abbey church to St Mary's. In November 1535 the notorious Visitors, Legh and Ap Rice, were sent by Cromwell to inspect the abbey. They reported that they could find little to fault, and concluded that there must have been a conspiracy of silence before their arrival. In 1535, it had a gross income of £2336 16s 11d, but after deductions, a net income of £1656 7s 3½d. Apart from the daily distribution of broken meat to the poor, the expenses of providing hospitality for all travellers and the various special feast day gifts, the abbey distributed nearly £400 a year to the poor. No other large English abbey gave so great a proportion of its income to this cause. In 1538 over 5000 marks in gold and silver were taken from the abbey by the King's agents, who reported that they had also removed a jewelled cross and various precious stones, but that they had left an adequate quantity of silver plate behind them for the needs of the community.

Bury St Edmunds Abbey was surrendered to the King on the 4 November 1539. The surrender document was signed by the abbot, the prior and forty-two monks. The last abbot, John Reeve, was awarded the very considerable pension of £333 6s 8d, but he died in Bury St Edmunds on 31 March 1540, never having claimed any of it. The value of the abbey at the Dissolution was considerable.

The abbey precinct was sold by the crown for £412 19s 4d, to John Eyer and transferred to Thomas Badby and, with the exception of the abbot's palace, was stripped of all valuable building material, the ruins then becoming a quarry for the townspeople. The abbot's palace survived as a house until 1720. In the seventeenth, eighteenth and early nineteenth centuries, a number of small houses were built into the west front of the abbey church. Some of these still survive.

A reconstruction of the west front by A B Whittingham

Description

ABBEY CHURCH

Although very extensively robbed, enough remains of the abbey church to give a reasonable impression of the scale of this great building. The church was among the few of its date built on the largest scale in this country, it being 505ft (154m) long or about 50ft (15m) longer than Norwich cathedral and some 12ft (3.6m) wider. The first of its kind in East Anglia, it exercised a strong influence on the development of the new style there.

East end and crypt

As was normal practice, the church was started at the east end. This was apsidal with an ambulatory of seven bays producing very narrow arches. They had round columns, as proved by part of a carved capital which was found. At the focal point of the apse stood the *shrine of St Edmund* placed behind the high altar near the shrines of Sts Jurmin and Botolph. There were two projecting semi-circular chapels with an elongated apsidal chapel between them. Below the presbytery was a crypt the sturdy round columns of which were over 6ft (1.8m) in diameter. Its plan is derived from St Augustine's, Canterbury, where the three chapels are equal, the arcades are cut straight through the walling, and there are narrow bays throughout, whereas here the elongated chapel, the round columns and the wider bays west of the apse are improvements. The walling of the chapels at the east end of this can still be seen. The north eastern one was dedicated to *St Anne*, the chapel above it in the main part of the church being dedicated to St Saba. Next in the centre below that of St Nicasius is the chapel of *St Mary* whose apse was still standing in 1745. On the south side, below that of St Peter, is the chapel of *St Robert*, whose tomb stood before the surviving altar of St Edward the Confessor, hence the crowns on some floor tiles. Its importance is shown by the stone seats below the adjoining aisle windows. Between the two other chapels was a *fair spring* whose water flowed into the trough behind and a projecting basin in front on a wide step. The crypt was four bays in length with a double row of narrow shafts between the main arcades carrying groined vaulting. The bays were separated by arches formed of a ring of unmoulded stones, and pieces of Saxon balusters were found embedded in the vaulting. Roman brick is occasionally used in the walling. The crypt was first lighted by narrow loop windows, each with an iron bar

up the middle. Three on the north which were obstructed by Canute's rotunda were left when the remaining ailse windows were enlarged in about 1250. In the chapels the small windows were left, one on the south preserving evidence that these were double-splayed between the square buttresses. The chapels were of three storeys, the uppermost series being entered from the triforium gallery.

Behind glass in St Robert's Chapel is a Tudor IHS between stars, for 'Jesus.' Remains of painted decoration in red were found on the west wall, and masonry pattern enclosing roses on the other walls. Twin stairs led down from the transepts, only that at the south west corner being excavated. The crypt was originally excavated in the eighteenth century, when part of the poet-monk Lydgate's tomb was found. It was re-excavated by the Ministry of Public Building and Works (now the Department of the Environment) which began work in 1957.

Choir

To sacrist Godfrey is due a sudden increase in the scale of the church and the greater sophistication of its detail. As has been stated already, he completed the central tower and part of the nave to the west of it. In the tower piers broken Roman brick is used in the mortar to strengthen the lower parts. To the east of the crossing is the base of a temporary wall which enclosed the presbytery so that the latter could be in use while the transepts and nave were built. Godfrey's work included the lengthening of the presbytery by one bay to incorporate the crypt entrances and to allow for the transept aisle. The bases of his piers remain on the west where each of his two semi-columns is wider, more closely spaced and bolder than in the earlier work. This north east pier of the crossing shows evidence for a 59ft (18m) crossing arch, 19ft (5.8m) triforium, 26ft (7.9m) arcade, groined aisle vaulting, and the position of the vaulting shafts. In the fifth bay stood the *choir altar* with steps up each side into the presbytery where Abbot Baldwin's tomb was over the end of the crypt. North and south were the upper doors of the choir leading into the aisles where steps descended westward into the transepts. Remains of low openings through the steps to light the crypt stairs may be seen; east of these stair-wells was space to pass down a few steps along the transept aisles to the chapels and vestries. West of the choir altar were *the stalls* facing each other under the tower and in the east part of the nave on the partly-surviving platform raised 2ft (0.6m) above the transepts. On the west was the pulpitum or screen containing the great door of the choir flanked by return stalls, and behind that the altar of the Holy Cross in the nave. The east end of the north triforium of the nave has slipped down and leans against the north west pier of the crossing.

Transepts and chapels

The crossing piers and also the north wall and centre window of the transept which replaced the Saxon timber nave are the conspicuous parts standing. There are traces of the turret stair, to the triforium chapels and upper parts, behind the north respond of this transept arcade. Each transept had one stout circular pier with a pair of semi-columns on the east to support one of the transverse arches across the aisle, as evidenced by a central joint on this side only of the base. When completed each arm of the crossing contained two rounded

The abbot's palace in c 1680 from the west, with the south side of the
Great Court above. From a drawing at the RIBA by
Edmund Prideaux, 1727

Ruins of y^e Abby of B

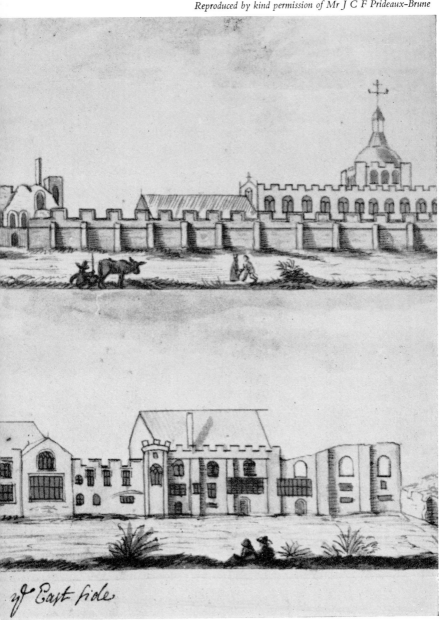

ye East side

but unbuttressed chapels, similar in size to those at the east end of the crypt. The outer chapel in the north transept was dedicated to St Martin, the adjoining one to St Mary. In 1275 this latter one was replaced by the present oblong *Lady Chapel*, which must have been entered through the original Norman arch, as the adjoining new arch would have been obstructed by the crypt stairs. Probably at this time the crypt windows adjoining the enlarged Lady Chapel were blocked, and an arcade constructed in front of them and in line with the east buttress which has later been extended so that it nearly blocks the next window of the crypt. A trace of the stone blocking still remains. Within the Lady Chapel lies part of the east arch of the crossing. It is of two orders, and shows a brick repair to the Norman work after the 1465 fire, and a new stone moulding on what was the east face. At the back the tunnel-vault over the clerestory passage is traceable. Because of the crypt the ambulatory leading to the three eastern chapels was raised about 4ft (1.2m) above the transept floor, and the same level would continue into a fourth chapel erected on the south before 1301 opposite the Lady Chapel and dedicated to *St Botolph*. It consisted of three bays flanking the aisle with a projection from the middle bay. It was linked to the shrine-keeper's house, whose successor is still in use. The chapel has been destroyed but part of its vaulted undercroft survives, blocking three of the crypt windows and originally reached by a staircase from above. In the *south transept*, the southern chapel was dedicated to St Nicholas, and the adjacent one to St John Evangelist. Out of this steps lead down north to a little room with an oven for baking holy bread. A later cistern blocks the steps. Above St John's Chapel was another at triforium level dedicated to St Giles. It was reached by the spiral stairs in the south west corner of the transept. The main south door led into the Great Cemetery. Before it stood the tomb of the Norman Count Alan of Brittany, founder of St Mary's Abbey, York, who had married the Conqueror's daughter and held East Anglian estates. He died in 1089.

Nave

West from the crossing the nave stretched on for twelve bays and then ended in a western transept. Flanking the west end on each side was a round-ended chapel. This work was finished before 1142, but was substantially increased in size by Abbot Samson who added three towers. From within the site of the nave, very little of this can be seen today, apart from the remains of some of the nave piers and two of the three blank thirteenth-century arches high on the north end of this transept, added when two Norman triforium arches were blocked for greater strength. Much of the west end has been destroyed and to see the most substantial remains of this it is necessary to proceed to the south-east of the present cathedral.

West front

The west front is marked by Abbot Anselm's three tall arches, once deeply recessed; they would have looked more imposing before the ground level was raised 4ft (1.2m) because of flooding. St Matthew's angel and the large carving of two devils thrusting a man into hell, now in Moyses Hall Museum, came probably from the jambs of the three west doors, being carved on two adjoining faces. As completed under Abbot Samson, this front was no less than 246 ft (75m) across, and in appearance was probably not unlike the west front at Ely Cathedral.

Samson built octagonal towers at each end of Anselm's front, adding buttresses and placing the stairs in an intervening angle in front of a lobby to link up with the chapels. On the north, the octagonal tower and adjoining part of the west front no longer exist, but the arch into the chapel and the three openings above from the gallery survive. The side-openings are narrow, one also being low to avoid the chapel vaulting. The highest wall surviving is part of the clerestory passage which has no openings into the north transept except two little vents. It seems possible that, in a way followed by Lincoln in *c* 1240, this clerestory or a lower passage in front was extended as a screen wall onto the octagonal towers, and faced with arcading on the west. It is highly probable that the central tower at the west end was similar to that at Ely. The remains show that Samson's tower had 11ft (3.3m) thick south and west walls and was set forward onto the front of the portico. There was a stair turret up both the front angles, the north of which remains at clerestory level and has a doorway askew into a passage over the side arch of the portico. There are signs of a turret each side of the north end of the transept. To strengthen the tower, the transept clerestories were rebuilt as a roof-space in the fifteenth century, apparently cut off by four-centered vaulting, the springers of which were found in the arch carrying each west clerestory passage.

Much of the detailed evidence here is concealed behind the façades of the later houses built into the west front.

MONASTIC BUILDINGS

Fairly extensive traces of the monastic buildings still survive at Bury. However, only those in the care of the State are described here. Readers are referred to the plan of the abbey in this handbook, and to the original article of which this text is a shortened version (see title page).

CLAUSTRAL BUILDINGS

The cloister lies north of the nave, and was laid out with its attendant buildings by Abbot Robert II (1102–07). The cloister walks were, however, rebuilt by Prior John Gosford at the end of the fourteenth century.

East range

This abuts the north wall of the north transept. Adjoining the transept is the *Inner Parlour*, where monks could go from the cloister for necessary conversation. East of this and approached by 'Trayledore' was the 'Trayle,' which led to the infirmary and the Chapel of St Andrew, as well as to the monks' cemetery and the sacrist's buildings. Its unusual length presumably accounts for its name. This parlour was widened and the *Chapter House*, where six abbots lie, was narrowed, lengthened and heavily buttressed by Richard de Neweport (sacrist 1213–29). Within the chapter house, at the east end, are the remains of the pulpitum. In the middle of the front edge of this is a socket for a metal dowel to hold the lectern, and beside it in a broken aumbrey, in which the Rule of St Benedict and the Martyrology were kept, was part of an iron chain by which the books were secured. In front a semi-circular step up to the pulpitum was found. A patch of alternately blue and yellow tiles laid diagonally remains near Samson's grave. The graves are those of Abbot Ording, 1148–56; Abbot Samson, 1182–1211; Abbot Richard de Insula, 1229–34; Abbot Henry de Rushbrook, 1234–48; Abbot Edmund de Walpole, 1248–56; and the grave next to the door with no coffin, that of Abbot Hugo I, 1157–80. Against the north wall is part of the surrounding stone bench. A quantity of coloured glass from the windows and carved stones was found here by excavators.

The adjoining *Dormitory Stairs* have been so robbed of ashlar that only the three containing walls are left. Beyond, a most unusual apse with Norman bases is contrived, because of the long transept, to give access to the *Warming House*, whose wall is splayed for the purpose, as well as to the *Treasury*, which has a pair of Norman courtyards protecting the windows. In the larger court is a stone water tank. It drained through a channel across the narrow court to the north which, having a sloped cobbled floor and a larger outlet (originally larger still and arched), seems intended for the disposal of waste water. Continuing north from the treasury are the remains of a long building. On the first floor of this was the monks' *Dormitory*, ending in the ruinous Queen's Chamber, while the rooms below were used for a variety of domestic purposes including storage.

BUILDINGS TO THE NORTH-EAST OF THE CHURCH

The principal route to the buildings lying to the east and north of the church was through Trayle. This led to the infirmary, which is largely under the modern tennis courts, passing through the little cloister, built by Prior John Gosford (1381 to post 1397), and between the vestry and the prior's house. Trayle where adjacent to the vestry shows evidence of Gosford's work which formed a single walk with no garth of its own. Here are remains of semi-octagonal shafts on bases consisting of an ogee above a round-edged splay, the shafts backed by chamfered wall-ribs, all standing on a double plinth which with the base made a neat design 18in (258mm) high. To the south of Trayle here lie the *Vestries*. These contained an altar of St Benedict and formed three sides of a small court drained under a connecting wing by a channel to a large rectangular sump further east. Part of a lancet survives next to a buttress. There are doorways to the Lady Chapel and from Trayle, some floor tiles remaining at the latter. Water was supplied by a well and two rainwater tanks. The sunk floor and bins in the north-east part are a later alteration.

The main approach to the prior's house was a covered way starting from Trayle-porch opposite the vestry and leading to his entrance gate. There it turned east, passing along the south of his entrance court and ended at his hall door. An alternative way led by a circuitous route to the garden outside the warming house and continued along the east side of the dormitory range to give access from the abbot's palace, the Great Court and the kitchens. Facing Trayle-porch is a much-burnt hearth below ground with a Norman wall of coursed flints running west from it. This seems to be part of the previous prior's hospice, as it certainly formed the north wall of a building destroyed to make way for the extended chapter house.

To the west of the prior's entrance court lies an enigmatic building, forming a sort of two-armed cloister. This was a two-storey structure, the upper floor being apparently the *Library*, while on the ground floor was the novices' school. The library was built by Abbot Curteys *c* 1430. Of his date may be the rounded angles here and in the circuitous passage. The entrance to the school was evidently in the east wing. A small room in the angle of the school has a round-headed culvert arch in a 3in (76mm) recess for a sluice door. On each side the recess ended, a little below the crown, in a stop to catch the projecting shoulders of the door and keep it level when lowered. The arch, tooled with a chisel, cannot be earlier than the time of Abbot Samson. It passes through a thin wall into the unexcavated north half of the building, and might be a device for flushing the drains when the stream from the west was not flowing fast enough.

South of the prior's entrance court and entered from it was the *Prior's Garden*. The wall of this abuts an enlarged shed built against the plinth of Trayle in one corner. One sump drains a small stone tank beyond the Trayle-porch, another with a domed top and keystone drained a pipe in the angle from the two pentice roofs, which protected the prior's approach to his house. A door from the garden to Trayle was later blocked for privacy.

Prior's house

This lies to the east of the dormitory and was presumably linked to the reredorter. The prior's house was remodelled by Prior John of Cambridge and repaired after damage when he was slain by the rebels in 1381. It retains his moulded jambs to the Hall door in the corner of his entrance-court. His, too, may be the extension, with a diagonal buttress, of the 1276 chapel to the east, which had a small chancel and a pair of stout buttresses at the angle of the nave adjoining a later rood stair turret. The chapel itself was on the upper floor. The later east end has a wall across the corner, flat at the back but curved in front, so probably there was a curved niche in both corners. The 1276 chapel was dedicated to St Stephen and St Edmund in substitution for two removed in extending the church; the earlier prior's chapel had been the round chapel of St Edmund on the site of the new Lady Chapel.

The hall has a clasping buttress of c 1210, and maintains the earlier width of Trayle before chapter house reconstruction allowed of its widening. Because of the chapel the east door of the screens passage is moved nearer to the site of the dais opposite a door to the infirmary. The evidence of Tudor bricks found in the hall suggests than an upper chamber may have been reconstructed late in its life. Its garderobe pit is south of Trayle, while the earlier drainage channel lies between the hall and the site of a staircase across the end. The butteries and kitchens are at the north end of the house. Bucks' view shows it had six lancets for the ground floor, the upper floor jettied each side of the chapel door, and a buttress supported the kitchen.

Infirmary

The infirmary lies askew parallel with the river approached by a vestibule down steps from Trayle. Next to a stone seat is the doorway to the infirmary hall, which retains the north respond of a row of piers down the middle and is mostly covered by the tennis courts. Between it and the monks' cemetery was a lighting area and then the continuation of Trayle to the sacrist's building further south.

East of the vestibule are the remains of the infirmary chapel of St Benedict, entered by the blocked door opposite Trayle and built as the abbot's chapel by Abbot Uvius (1020–44). Part of its east wall survives outside the fence, and shows traces of a barrel vault running unexpectedly north and south. This suggests a plan with a narrow barrel-vaulted aisle surrounding a short clerestoried nave, two bays long by one bay wide under whose arches four early Abbots were buried. In the north wall is a blocked door with flint rear jambs leading to the site of the Saxon abbot's lodging. A tower stood west of the chapel with the Saxon chapter house behind it. The Normans added an infirmary chapel of St Michael, entered from the east end of the south aisle and now represented by two lumps; one of which, with a string-course, supports the Saxon east wall.

West of the infirmary chapel the vestibule incorporates a hall with a south aisle. A transitional circular base of c 1180 with well-carved angle

spurs identifies this as the New Infirmary completed under Abbot Samson. The hall, perhaps three bays long, was presently curtailed by a double-stairs over a door and converted into a vestibule by Prior Gosford (1381–97), witness the plinth mould (of a wall-arch?) next to the entrance. This entrance and the adjoining stairs were the main approach to the infirmary, the other stairs and door opposite doors into the prior's chapel and hall must have been for his use. The intervening small irregular court drained under Trayle, which was also called the little cloister next to the infirmary chapel.

Reredorter and beyond

To the north of the prior's house stand some detached buttresses, which mark the north side of the thirteenth-century reredorter. One of a

The Norman gate tower

row of ashlar drainage shafts, discharging into an arch, spaced about every 4ft (1.2m), is visible between the unevenly spaced buttresses and the wall. Originally there was a row of arches, but they were blocked up and only the flint blockings survive. Probably a channel was formed above them instead when the buttresses were added. Possibly the raising of the mill-stream caused the rebuilding of the Norman reredorter, but the new plan with shafts instead of a channel gives a wider undercroft. A fragment of its vaulting survives in the angle.

Nearer the river are the foundations of a little building, with a fireplace and a well, which may have housed the prior's two esquires. The siting of this building is due to a cobbled way past its south west side leading from the Great Court and the abbot's garden to the vineyard across the river.

To the north of the reredorter, and now forming part of the public park, lay the abbot's garden centering on the Queen's chamber, now ruinous. Its north wall terminates in the conspicuous hexagonal dovecote with drainage culvert, while its southern companion protected the drain from the reredorter. The precince wall is carried across the River Lark on the abbot's bridge. This three-arch bridge dates from the early part of the thirteenth century and has a procession way on the inside, which at first rose above the taller arches, where there are remains of an offset. In the fourteenth century, however, the inner arches and procession way were lowered for convenience in working the portcullises the grooves of which survive against its inner face. At the same time the gables and flying buttresses on the exterior cutwaters were added to provide a plank footbridge beside the ford. In the adjoining corner is a Tudor lobby connecting with the footbridge and with All Soul's Gate, the east gate of the town which came under the abbot's jurisdiction, so that the gateporter could also operate the portcullises guarding access by water under the Abbot's Bridge. The wall-face has been set back for the doorway cut through the last buttress.

ABBEY GATEWAYS

The two great gateways are the best preserved of all the buildings of the abbey. The survival of their ashlar and decoration gives an excellent idea of the quality of the stonework of which only fragments remain elsewhere in the abbey.

Norman tower

This dates from 1120–48 and was designed to be both a gateway to the abbey church and a belfry to the neighbouring church of St James. It still fulfills this latter function. This church was founded by Abbot Anselm instead of making a pilgrimage to St James at Compostella. The tower, also known as the tower of St James, has three windows on each face. The tympanum of the west arch was removed in 1789 to let hay carts through. The slab which formerly showed matrices of two bells and two melting-pots on tripods, commemorating one of the Bury bell-founders, has been placed at the original ground level.

Great Gate

This gave access to the Great Court and to the abbot's palace, and was probably always the most imposing building in the court. Coats of arms in the entrance show that it was built after 1327 when Henry, the King's cousin, became Duke of Lancaster, and before 1346 when Edward III began to use the quartered coat. The coats are: 1 Edward III; 2 destroyed; his uncles, 3 John of Eltham, and 4 Thomas Brotherton, Earl of Norfolk; 6 their cousin, Henry of Lancaster; with 5 Edward the Confessor. These, with other coats destroyed, apparently represent donors and benefactors. Flamboyant tracery in the wall-panels of the interior, and an early instance of perpendicular design suggest that one of the royal master-masons was at work here. The upper storey was, however, built by John Lavenham, sacrist after 1353–c 1384. It has lost the two octagonal turrets which capped the two stairs. It is planned with a watch room, in which the portcullis gear was worked, over the outer hall. Over the inner hall, which also has lost its vaulting, the room for the guards has large windows, a fireplace on the south and on the north a garderobe whose shute is backed by another for the stableman on the adjoining first floor. Below the main rooms, linking the stairs is a passage over the gate with slits commanding both halls. Externally the gateway combines provision for statuary, to display the ideal for which the abbey stood, with arrow-slits behind the statues should force again be needed to control the town, for the royal arm behind the abbey was strong enough to prevent the town acquiring self-government till after the abbey had been dissolved.

Glossary

AISLE	Part of church on either side of nave or chancel, etc.
ASHLAR	Squared blocks of stone.
AUMBREY	Wall-cupboard or locker.
BAY	Structural division of the length of a building or roof.
BLACK HOSTRY	Local name for guest hall for Benedictine monks.
CAMERA	Room, lodging or house, especially of an official.
CHAPTER HOUSE	Room in which the brethren met daily for monastic business, when an article or chapter of the monastic rule was read.
CLERESTORY	Row of windows set above the line of the aisle roof and admitting light to the central part of church.
CLOISTER	An enclosure consisting of four covered walks, the centre of monastic life, round a 'garth,' plot or garden; a 'little cloister' rarely has more than two covered walks, and here only one with no garth, as the infirmary garden was on the far side of the infirmary.
CROSSING	Central space where east-west axis of church is crossed by north-south axis of transepts.
GARDEROBE	Latrine or privy.
NAVE	Part of church extending west from crossing.
PENTICE	Penthouse or lean-to.
PRESBYTERY	Eastern part of church containing principal altar.
PULPITUM	A raised platform from which to speak, especially one forming a partition or screen between nave and choir.
QUIRE OR CHOIR	Part of church between presbytery and nave, containing stalls where the monks sat to sing the offices.
REFECTORY	Dining hall.

REREDORTER	Building containing latrines.
RESPOND	Half-pier bonded into a wall and supporting one end of an arch.
SPLAY	The slanting reveal of window or doorway.
TRAYLE	Local name for passage from cloister to the cemetery.
TRIFORIUM	Row of arches into roof-space over aisle, producing three-tier sides to central parts of church.
TRANSEPT	Transverse part of a cruciform church, set at right angles to the main axis.
WARMING HOUSE	Only room in which a fire was allowed round which the brethren might warm themselves.

Printed in Scotland by Her Majesty's Stationery Office at HMSO Press, Edinburgh
Dd 595630 K124 6/78 (15472)